T0031156

JIMMY'S BLUES AND OTHER POEMS

A NOTE ON THE TEXT:

We have honored James Baldwin's own original typographical and grammatical preferences in this volume, both in presenting the poems from *Jimmy's Blues* exactly as they were originally printed and in the poems taken from the privately printed, limited-edition volume, *Gypsy*, as Baldwin had determined shortly before his death. While this has resulted in formatting inconsistencies within this volume, we believe it is important to reflect his own choices.

JIMMY'S
BLUES
AND OTHER POEMS

JAMES BALDWIN

WITH AN INTRODUCTION
BY NIKKY FINNEY

Beacon Press
Boston

Beacon Press
Boston, Massachusetts
www.beacon.org

Beacon Press books
are published under the auspices of the
Unitarian Universalist Association of Congregations.

26 25 24 23   14 13 12 11 10

This book is printed on acid-free paper that meets the uncoated paper
ANSI/NISO specifications for permanence as revised in 1992.

Text design by Gabi Anderson and Ruth Maassen

Library of Congress Cataloging-in-Publication Data

Baldwin, James, 1924–1987
  [Poems. Selections]
  Jimmy's blues and other poems / James Baldwin ; with an introduc-
tion by Nikky Finney.
      pages cm
  ISBN 978-0-8070-8486-1 (paperback : acid-free paper)—ISBN 978-
0-8070-8487-8 (ebook)
  I. Finney, Nikky. II. Title.
  PS3552.A45A6 2014
  811'.54—dc23
                          2013041958

JIMMY'S BLUES AND OTHER POEMS

CONTENTS

Introduction by Nikky Finney   ix

JIMMY'S BLUES

Staggerlee wonders   3
Song (for Skip)   20
Munich, Winter 1973 (for Y.S.)   26
The giver (for Berdis)   30
3.00 a.m. (for David)   31
The darkest hour   32
Imagination   32
Confession   33
Le sporting-club de Monte Carlo (for Lena Horne)   40
Some days (for Paula)   41
Conundrum (on my birthday) (for Rico)   44
Christmas carol   46
A lady like landscapes (for Simone Signoret)   52
Guilt, Desire and Love   53
Death is easy (for Jefe)   55
Mirrors (for David)   58
A Lover's Question   60
Inventory/On Being 52   64
Amen   71

OTHER POEMS

Gypsy   75

Song For The Shepherd Boy   85

For A.   87

For EARL   89

Untitled   91

BALLAD (for Yoran)   92

PLAYING BY EAR, PRAYING FOR RAIN: THE POETRY OF JAMES BALDWIN

Baldwin was never afraid to say it. He made me less afraid to say it too.

The air of the Republic was already rich with him when I got here. James Arthur Baldwin, the most salient, sublime, and consequential American writer of the twentieth century, was in the midst of publishing his resolute and prophetic essays and novels: *Go Tell It on the Mountain* (1953), *The Amen Corner* (1954), *Notes of a Native Son* (1955), and *Giovanni's Room* (1956). I arrived on planet earth in the middle of his personal and relentless assault on white supremacy and his brilliant, succinct understanding of world and American history. In every direction I turned, my ears filled a little more with what he always had to say. His words, his spirit, mattered to me. Black, gay, bejeweled, eyes like orbs searching, dancing, calling *a spade a spade*, in magazines and on the black-and-white TV of my youth. Baldwin, deep in thought and pulling drags from his companion cigarettes, looking his and our danger in the face and never backing down. My worldview was set in motion by this big, bold heart who understood that he had to leave his America in order to be. Baldwin was dangerous to everybody who had anything to hide. Baldwin was also the priceless inheritance to anybody looking for manumission from who they didn't want or have to be. Gracious and tender, a man who had no idea or concept of his place, who nurtured conversation with Black Panthers and the white literati all in the same afternoon. So powerful and controversial was his name that one minute it was there on the speaker's list for the great August 28, 1963, March on Washington for Jobs and Freedom, and then, poof, it was off. The country might have been ready to march for things they believed all God's children should have in this life, but there were people, richly mis-educated by the Republic, who were not ready for James Baldwin to bring truth in those searing ways he always brought truth to the multitudes.

The eldest of nine, a beloved son of Harlem, his irreverent pride and trust in his own mind, his soul (privately and sometimes publicly warring), all of who he was and believed himself to be, was exposed in his first person, unlimited voice, not for sale, but vulnerable to the Republic. Baldwin's proud sexuality, and his unwillingness to censor his understanding that sex was a foundational part of this life even in the puritanical Republic and therefore should be written, unclothed, not whispered about, not roped off in some back room, informed all of his work, but especially his poetry. Uninviting Baldwin was often the excuse for the whitewashing of his urgent and necessary brilliance from both the conservative Black community and from whites who had never heard such a dark genius display such rich and sensory antagonism for them. Into the microphone of the world Baldwin leaned—never afraid to say it.

Only once did I see James Baldwin live and in warm, brilliant person; it was 1984, a packed house at the University of California at Berkeley. I was thirty-seven, he was sixty, and we would never meet. None of us there that night, standing shoulder to shoulder, pushed to the edge of our seats, knew that this was our last embrace with him, that we would only have him walking among us for three more years. I remember the timbre of his voice. Steadfast. Smoky. Serene. His words fell on us like a good rain. A replenishing we badly needed. All of us standing, sitting, spread out before this wise, sharp-witted, all-seeing man.

I had *met* James Baldwin by way of his "Sweet Lorraine," a seventeen-hundred-and seventy-six-word loving manifesto to his friend and comrade, the playwright Lorraine Hansberry. Hansberry died from cancer at the age of thirty-four, soon after her great work, *To Be Young, Gifted, and Black,* yanked the apron and head rag off the institution of the American theater, Broadway, 1959. Baldwin's intimate remembrance became the introduction to the book of the same name, a book that, as a girl of fourteen, I was highly uncomfortable ever letting out of my sight. I was the Black girl dreaming of a writing life and Hansberry, the Black woman carving one out. Hansberry had given me two atomic oars to zephyr me further upstream: *I am a writer. I am going to write.* After her untimely death, I had a palpable need to still see and feel her in the world. Baldwin's lush remembrance brought her to me in powerful living dimension. His way of seeing her, of remembering what was important about her, helped her stay with me.

I had needed Hansberry to set my determination forward for my journey. And I needed Baldwin to teach me about the power of rain.

Baldwin wrote poetry throughout his life. He wrote with an engaged, layered, facile hand. The idea being explored first cinched, then stretched out, with just enough tension to bring the light in. His language: informal, inviting; his ideas from the four corners of the earth, beginning, always, with love:

> *No man can have a harlot*
> *for a lover*
> *nor stay in bed forever*
> *with a lie.*
> *He must rise up*
> *and face the morning sky*
> *and himself, in the mirror*
> *of his lover's eye.*
> ("A Lover's Question")

Baldwin's images carry their weight and we, the reader, carry their consequence. In one turn of phrase and line, something lies easy in repose; in the next, he is telling the Lord what to do; the words jump, fall in line, with great and marching verve:

> *Lord,*
> > *when you send the rain,*
> > *think about it, please,*
> > *a little?*
>
> *Do*
> > *not get carried away*
> > *by the sound of falling water,*
> > *the marvelous light*
> > *on the falling water.*

> *I*
>
> *am beneath that water.*
> *It falls with great force*
> *and the light*
> Blinds
> *me to the light.*
>
> ("Untitled")

Baldwin wrote as the words instructed, never allowing the critics of the Republic to tell him how or how not. They could listen in or they could ignore him, but he was never their boy, writing something they wanted to hear. He fastidiously handed that empty caricature of a Black writer back to them, tipping his hat, turning back to his sweet Harlem alley for more juice.

James Baldwin, as poet, was incessantly paying attention and always leaning into the din and hum around him, making his poems from his notes of what was found there, making his outlines, his annotations, doing his jotting down, writing from the mettle and marginalia of his life, giving commentary, scribbling, then dispatching out to the world what he knew and felt about that world. James Baldwin, as poet, was forever licking the tip of his pencil, preparing for more calculations, more inventory, moving, counting each letter being made inside the abacus of the poem. James Baldwin, as poet, never forgot what he had taught me in that seventeen-hundred-and-seventy-six-word essay—to remember where one came from. So many of the poems are dedicated back to someone who perhaps had gone the distance, perhaps had taught him about the rain: *for David* (x3), *for Jefe, for Lena Horne, for Rico, for Berdis, for Y.S.*

When the writer Cecil Brown went to see James Baldwin in Paris in the summer of 1982, he found him "busy working on a collection of poems," quite possibly these poems. Brown reports that Baldwin would work on a poem for a while and then stop from time to time to read one aloud to him. "Staggerlee wonders" was one of those poems, and "Staggerlee wonders" opens *Jimmy's Blues*, the collection he published in 1983. The poem begins with indefatigable might, setting the tone and temperature for everything else in this volume, as well as the sound and sense found throughout Baldwin's *oeuvre*. "Baldwin read to me from the poem with great humor and laughter," Brown wrote in his book *Stagolee Shot Billy*.

> He felt that Black men in America, as the most obvious targets of white oppression, had to love each other, to warn each other, and to communicate with each other if they were to escape being defined only in reaction to that oppression. They had to seek and find in their own tradition the human qualities that white men, through their unrelenting brutality, had lost.

I do not believe James Baldwin can be wholly read without first understanding white men and their penchant for tyranny and "unrelenting brutality." If you read Baldwin without this truth, you will mistake Baldwin's use of the word *nigger* as how he saw himself, instead of that long-suffering character, imagined, invented, and marched to the conveyor belt as if it was the hanging tree, by the founding fathers of the Republic, in order that they might hold on for as long as possible to "the very last white country the world will ever see" (Baldwin, "Notes on the House of Bondage").

I always wonder
what they think the niggers are doing
while they, the pink and alabaster pragmatists,
are containing
Russia
and defining and re-defining and re-aligning
China,
nobly restraining themselves, meanwhile,
from blowing up that earth
("Staggerlee wonders")

With prophetic understanding, harmony, and swing, creating his own style and using his own gauges to navigate the journey, Baldwin often wrote counter-metrically, reflecting his African, Southern, Harlem, and Paris roots. "What do you like about Emily Dickinson?" he was once asked in a *Paris Review* interview. His answer: "Her use of language . . . Her solitude, as well, and the style of that solitude. There is something very moving and in the best sense funny."

James Baldwin made laughter of a certain style even as he reported the lies of the Republic. He was so aware of that other face so necessary in this life, that face that was present in all the best human dramatic monologues, the high historic Black art of laughing to keep from crying. He knew that without the blues there would be no jazz. Just as Baldwin dropped you into the fire, there he was extinguishing it with laughter.

Neither (incidentally)
has anyone discussed the Bomb with the niggers:
the incoherent feeling is, the less
the nigger knows about the Bomb, the better:
the lady of the house
smiles nervously in your direction
as though she had just been overheard
discussing family, or sexual secrets,
and changes the subject to Education,
or Full Employment, or the Welfare rolls,
the smile saying, Don't be dismayed.
We know how you feel. You can trust us.
("Staggerlee wonders")

Baldwin wrote poetry because he felt close to this partic-
ular form and this particular way of saying. Poetry helped
thread his ideas from the essays, to the novels, to the love
letters, to the book reviews, stitching images and feeling
into music, back to his imagination. From the beginning
of his life to the very end, I believe Baldwin saw himself
more poet than anything else: The way he cared about
language. The way he believed language should work. The
way he understood what his friend and mentor, the great
American painter Beauford Delaney, had taught him—to
look close, not just at the water but at the oil sitting there
on top of the water. This reliable witnessing eye was the
true value of seeing the world for what it really was and not
for what someone reported, from afar, that it was.

When Baldwin took off for Switzerland in 1952, he car-
ried recordings by Bessie Smith, and he would often fall
asleep listening to them, taking her in like the sweet Black

poetry she sang. It must have been her *Baby don't worry, I got you* voice and their shared blues that pushed him through to finish *Go Tell It on the Mountain* in three months, after struggling with the story for ten years. Whenever Baldwin abandoned the music of who he was and how that sound was made, he momentarily lost his way. When he lost his way, I believe it was poetry that often brought him back. I believe he wrote poetry throughout his life because poetry brought him back to the music, back to the rain. The looking close. The understanding and presence of the oil on top of the water. Compression. Precision. The metaphor. The riff and shout. The figurative. The high notes. The blues. The reds. The whites. This soaking up. That treble clef. Bass. Baldwin could access it all—and did—with poetry.

> *He was standing at the bath-room mirror,*
> *shaving,*
> *had just stepped out of the shower,*
> *naked,*
> *balls retracted, prick limped out of the*
> *small,*
> *morning hard-on,*
> *thinking of nothing but foam and steam,*
> *when the bell*
> *rang.*
> ("Gypsy")

Baldwin integrated the power of sex and the critical dynamics of the family with ease. He spoke often and passionately about the preciousness of children, the beloved ones. He never hid from any language that engaged the human conundrum, refusing to allow the narrow world to deny him, Black, bejeweled, Harlem insurgent, demanding to add his poetic voice to all others of his day. Sometimes employing a simple rhyme scheme and rhythm, as in "The giver," a poem dedicated to his mother, Berdis, and then, again, giving rise to poetic ear-play in "Imagination."

> *Imagination*
> *creates the situation,*
> *and then, the situation*
> *creates imagination.*
>
> *It may, of course,*
> *be the other way around:*
> *Columbus was discovered*
> *by what he found.*

In several of his last interviews you hear James Baldwin repeat something you know is on his mind: "The older you get, the more you realize the little you know." This Black man of the Black diaspora, born in 1924, the same year that J. Edgar Hoover was appointed the new director of the FBI, forever taking stock of his life as it unfolded:

> *My progress report*
> *concerning my journey to the palace of wisdom*
> *is discouraging.*
> *I lack certain indispensable aptitudes.*
> *Furthermore, it appears*
> *that I packed the wrong things.*
> ("Inventory/On Being 52")

Jimmy's Blues and Other Poems is being published in what would have been Baldwin's—our loving, long-cussed, steadfast witness in this world's—ninetieth year. These poems represent the notations, permutations, the Benjamin Banneker–like wonderings of a curious heart devoted to exposing tyranny, love, and the perpetual historical lies of the Republic.

In a 1961 interview, Studs Terkel asks Jimmy Baldwin after Baldwin's first twenty years as a writer, *"Who are you now?"* Baldwin answers,

> *Who, indeed. I may be able to tell you who I am, but I am also discovering who I am not. I want to be an honest man. And I want to be a good writer. I don't know if one ever gets to be what one wants to be. You just have to play it by ear, and pray for rain.*

He never rested on any fame, award, or success. He didn't linger in the noisy standing ovation we gave him that night in California. He didn't need the poison of whatever it meant "to be famous" pounding at his door. Refusing to stand in any shadow, Baldwin understood that any light on his life might open some doors, but in the end it was his pounding heart, caring and remaining focused on the community, that had always defined him, that mattered. In his work he remained devoted to exposing more and more the ravages of poverty and invisibility on Black and poor people. He loved it when people came to talk and listen to his stories, his rolling laughter, and consented to be transformed by his various arenas of language and his many forms of expression. These were friends and strangers, artists, who only wanted to feel him say what he had to say.

People hungry to hear James Baldwin unabridged, before the night got too late and his devotion would make him rise and return him to the aloneness of his work, in that space he called his "torture chamber," his study. Baldwin told the *Paris Review*, "Every form is different, no one is easier than another. They all kick your ass." There on his desk, the next page of "ass kicking" awaited.

In 1963, James Baldwin visited San Francisco. The journey was amazingly caught on fuzzy black-and-white, educational TV in the KQED documentary *Take This Hammer*. One morning during his visit he found himself speaking with a group of frustrated young Black men standing there on the street. One of the young men reports, "There will never be a Negro president." Baldwin asks him why he believes this. The young man responds, hardly catching his breath: "We can't even get a job. How can we be president if we can't even get a job?" You see Baldwin on camera move instantly closer to the storm raging from their ring of eyes to his. You see and feel the fire in their faces and in his. He knows this gathering storm well. He can hear the sounds of the thunder gathering deep in his ear. He has seen this same kind of lightning flash, hit, and burn down whole countries, whole neighborhoods, whole city corners, with their standing communities of young Black men. He himself has been soaked in this despair before. His inclination is to lead them away from the storm, but he's in the storm too, and he won't lie to them like everybody else has lied. He looks at them with great love. He can see the oil in the water on their cheeks. "There will be a Negro president," Baldwin says calmly. "But it will not be the country that we are sitting in now." It begins to rain. It doesn't really, but that's what the scene feels like to me through the camera's grainy lens, fifty years away from Baldwin and that circle of beautiful and young Black men wanting what other young men wanted, there on that San Francisco street. It begins to rain, at first a light drizzle and next a pounding torrent, great sheets of great water, slanted and falling down from the open sky. Baldwin was never afraid to say it in his novels, in his essays, and in his poetry—because Baldwin saw us long before we saw ourselves.

—*Nikky Finney*

JIMMY'S
BLUES

Staggerlee wonders

1

I always wonder
what they think the niggers are doing
while they, the pink and alabaster pragmatists,
are containing
Russia
and defining and re-defining and re-aligning
China,
nobly restraining themselves, meanwhile,
from blowing up that earth
which they have already
blasphemed into dung:
the gentle, wide-eyed, cheerful
ladies, and their men,
nostalgic for the noble cause of Vietnam,
nostalgic for noble causes,
aching, nobly, to wade through the blood of savages—
ah—!
Uncas shall never leave the reservation,
except to purchase whisky at the State Liquor Store.
The Panama Canal shall remain forever locked:
there is a way around every treaty.
We will turn the tides of the restless
Caribbean,

the sun will rise, and set
on our hotel balconies as we see fit.
The natives will have nothing to complain about,
indeed, they will begin to be grateful,
will be better off than ever before.
They will learn to defer gratification
and save up for things, like we do.

Oh, yes. They will.
We have only to make an offer
they cannot refuse.

This flag has been planted on the moon:
it will be interesting to see
what steps the moon will take to be revenged
for this quite breathtaking presumption.
This people
masturbate in winding sheets.
They have hacked their children to pieces.
They have never honoured a single treaty
made with anyone, anywhere.
The walls of their cities
are as foul as their children.
No wonder their children come at them with knives.
Mad Charlie man's son was one of their children,
had got his shit together
by the time he left kindergarten,
and, as for Patty, heiress of all the ages,

she had the greatest vacation
of any heiress, anywhere:

Golly-gee, whillikens, Mom, real guns!
and they come with a real big, black funky stud, too:
oh, Ma! he's making eyes at me!

Oh, noble Duke Wayne,
be careful in them happy hunting grounds.
They say the only good Indian
is a dead Indian,
but what I say is,
you can't be too careful, you hear?
Oh, towering Ronnie Reagan,
wise and resigned lover of redwoods,
deeply beloved, winning man-child of the yearning
    Republic,
from diaper to football field to Warner Brothers
        sound-stages,
be thou our grinning, gently phallic, Big Boy of all the ages!

Salt peanuts, salt peanuts,
for dear hearts and gentle people,
and cheerful, shining, simple Uncle Sam!

Nigger, read this and run!
Now, if you can't read,
run anyhow!

From Manifest Destiny
(*Cortez, and all his men*
silent upon a peak in Darien)
to A Decent Interval,
and the chopper rises above Saigon,
abandoning the noble cause
and the people we have made ignoble
and whom we leave there, now, to die,
one moves, With All Deliberate Speed,
to the South China Sea, and beyond,
where millions of new niggers
await glad tidings!

No, said the Great Man's Lady,
I'm against abortion.
I always feel that's killing somebody.
Well, what about capital punishment?
I think the death penalty helps.

That's right.
Up to our ass in niggers
on Death Row.

Oh, Susanna,
don't you cry for me!

2

Well, I guess what the niggers
is supposed to be doing
is putting themselves in the path
of that old sweet chariot
and have it swing down and carry us home.

That would *help*, as they say,
and they got ways
of sort of nudging the chariot.
They still got influence
with Wind and Water,
though they in for some surprises
with Cloud and Fire.

My days are not their days.
My ways are not their ways.
I would not think of them,
one way or the other,
did not they so grotesquely
block the view
between me and my brother.

And, so, I always wonder:
can blindness be desired?
Then, what must the blinded eyes have seen
to wish to see no more!

For, I have seen,
in the eyes regarding me,
or regarding my brother,
have seen, deep in the farthest valley
of the eye, have seen
a flame leap up, then flicker and go out,
have seen a veil come down,
leaving myself, and the other,
alone in that cave
which every soul remembers, and
out of which, desperately afraid,
I turn, turn, stagger, stumble out,
into the healing air,
fall flat on the healing ground,
singing praises, counselling
my heart, my soul, to praise.

What is it that this people
cannot forget?

Surely, they cannot be so deluded
as to imagine that their crimes
are original?

There is nothing in the least original
about the fiery tongs to the eyeballs,
the sex torn from the socket,
the infant ripped from the womb,

the brains dashed out against rock,
nothing original about Judas,
or Peter, or you or me: nothing:
we are liars and cowards all,
or nearly all, or nearly all the time:
for we also ride the lightning,
answer the thunder, penetrate whirlwinds,
curl up on the floor of the sun,
and pick our teeth with thunderbolts.

Then, perhaps they imagine
that their crimes are not crimes?

Perhaps.
Perhaps that is why they cannot repent,
why there is no possibility of repentance.
Manifest Destiny is a hymn to madness,
feeding on itself, ending
(when it ends) in madness:
the action is blindness and pain,
pain bringing a torpor so deep
that every act is willed,
is desperately forced,
is willed to be a blow:
the hand becomes a fist,
the prick becomes a club,
the womb a dangerous swamp,
the hope, and fear, of love

—9—

is acid in the marrow of the bone.
No, their fire is not quenched,
nor can be: the oil feeding the flames
being the unadmitted terror of the wrath of God.

Yes. But let us put it in another,
less theological way:
though theology has absolutely nothing to do
with what I am trying to say.
But the moment God is mentioned
theology is summoned
to buttress or demolish belief:
an exercise which renders belief irrelevant
and adds to the despair of Fifth Avenue
on any afternoon,
the people moving, homeless, through the city,
praying to find sanctuary before the sky
and the towers come tumbling down,
before the earth opens, as it does in *Superman.*
They know that no one will appear
to turn back time,
they know it, just as they know
that the earth has opened before
and will open again, just as they know
that their empire is falling, is doomed,
nothing can hold it up, nothing.
We are not talking about belief.

3

I wonder how they think
the niggers made, make it,
how come the niggers are still here.
But, then, again, I don't think they dare
to think of that: no:
I'm fairly certain they don't think of that at all.

Lord,
I watch the alabaster lady of the house,
with Beulah.
Beulah about sixty, built four-square,
biceps like Mohammed Ali,
she at the stove, fixing biscuits,
scrambling eggs and bacon, fixing coffee,
pouring juice, and the lady of the house,
she say, she don't know *how*
she'd get along without Beulah
and Beulah just silently grunts,
I reckon you don't,
and keeps on keeping on
and the lady of the house say,
She's just like one of the family,
and Beulah turns, gives me a look,
sucks her teeth and rolls her eyes
in the direction of the lady's back, and
keeps on keeping on.

While they are containing
Russia
and entering onto the quicksand of
China
and patronizing
Africa,
and calculating
the Caribbean plunder, and
the South China Sea booty,
the niggers are aware that no one has discussed
anything at all with the niggers.

Well. Niggers don't own nothing,
got no flag, even our names
are hand-me-downs
and you don't change that
by calling yourself X:
sometimes that just makes it worse,
like obliterating the path that leads back
to whence you came, and
to where you can begin.
And, anyway, none of this changes the reality,
which is, for example, that I do not want my son
to die in Guantanamo,
or anywhere else, for that matter,
serving the Stars and Stripes.
(I've *seen* some stars.
I *got* some stripes.)

Neither (incidentally)
has anyone discussed the Bomb with the niggers:
the incoherent feeling is, the less
the nigger knows about the Bomb, the better:
the lady of the house
smiles nervously in your direction
as though she had just been overheard
discussing family, or sexual secrets,
and changes the subject to Education,
or Full Employment, or the Welfare rolls,
the smile saying, *Don't be dismayed.*
We know how you feel. You can trust us.

Yeah. I would like to believe you.
But we are not talking about belief.

4

The sons of greed, the heirs of plunder,
are approaching the end of their journey:
it is amazing that they approach without wonder,
as though they have, themselves, become
that scorched and blasphemed earth,
the stricken buffalo, the slaughtered tribes,
the endless, virgin, bloodsoaked plain,
the famine, the silence, the children's eyes,
murder masquerading as salvation, seducing

every democratic eye,
the mouths of truth and anguish choked with cotton,
rape delirious with the fragrance of magnolia,
the hacking of the fruit of their loins to pieces,
hey! the tar-baby sons and nephews, the high-yaller
    nieces,
and Tom's black prick hacked off
to rustle in the crinoline,
to hang, heaviest of heirlooms,
between the pink and alabaster breasts
of the Great Man's Lady,
or worked into the sash at the waist
of the high-yaller Creole bitch, or niece,
a chunk of shining brown-black satin,
staring, staring, like the single eye of God:

creation yearns to re-create a time
when we were able to recognize a crime.

Alas,
my stricken kinsmen,
the party is over:
there have never been any white people,
anywhere: the trick was accomplished with mirrors—
look: where is your image now?
where your inheritance,
on what rock stands this pride?

Oh,
I counsel you,
leave History alone.
She is exhausted,
sitting, staring into her dressing-room mirror,
and wondering what rabbit, now,
to pull out of what hat,
and seriously considering retirement,
even though she knows her public
dare not let her go.

She must change.
Yes. History must change.
A slow, syncopated
relentless music begins
suggesting her re-entry,
transformed, virginal as she was,
in the Beginning, untouched,
as the Word was spoken,
before the rape which debased her
to be the whore of multitudes, or,
as one might say, before she became the Star,
whose name, above our title,
carries the Show, making History the patsy,
responsible for every flubbed line,
every missed cue, responsible for the life
and death, of all bright illusions
and dark delusions,

Lord, History is weary
of her unspeakable liaison with Time,
for Time and History
have never seen eye to eye:
Time laughs at History
and time and time and time again
Time traps History in a lie.

But we always, somehow, managed
to roar History back onstage
to take another bow,
to justify, to sanctify
the journey until now.

Time warned us to ask for our money back,
and disagreed with History
as concerns colours white and black.
Not only do we come from further back,
but the light of the Sun
marries all colours as one.

Kinsmen,
I have seen you betray your Saviour
(it is *you* who call Him Saviour)
so many times, and
I have spoken to Him about you,
behind your back.
Quite a lot has been going on

behind your back, and,
if your phone has not yet been disconnected,
it will soon begin to ring:
informing you, for example, that a whole generation,
in Africa, is about to die,
and a new generation is about to rise,
and will not need your bribes,
or your persuasions, any more:
nor your morality. Nor the plundered gold—
Ah! Kinsmen, if I could make you see
the crime is not what you have done to me!
It is you who are blind,
you, bowed down with chains,
you, whose children mock you, and seek another
master,
you, who cannot look man or woman or child in the
eye,
whose sleep is blank with terror,
for whom love died long ago,
somewhere between the airport and the safe-deposit
box,
the buying and selling of rising or falling stocks,
you, who miss Zanzibar and Madagascar and Kilimanjaro
and lions and tigers and elephants and zebras
and flying fish and crocodiles and alligators and
leopards
and crashing waterfalls and endless rivers,
flowers fresher than Eden, silence sweeter than the

grace of God,
passion at every turning, throbbing in the bush,
thicker, oh, than honey in the hive,
dripping
dripping
opening, welcoming, aching from toe to bottom
to spine,
sweet heaven on the line
to last forever, yes,
but, now,
rejoicing ends, man, a price remains to pay,
your innocence costs too much
and we can't carry you on our books
or our backs, any longer: baby,
find another Eden, another apple tree,
somewhere, if you can,
and find some other natives, somewhere else,
to listen to you bellow
till you come, just like a man,
but we don't need you,
are sick of being a fantasy to feed you,
and of being the principal accomplice to your
crime:
for, it is *your* crime, now, the cross to which you
cling,
your Alpha and Omega for everything.

Well (others have told you)

your clown's grown weary, the puppet master
is bored speechless with this monotonous disaster,
and is long gone, does not belong to you,
any more than my woman, or my child,
ever belonged to you.

During this long travail
our ancestors spoke to us, and we listened,
and we tried to make you hear life in our song
but now it matters not at all to me
whether you know what I am talking about—or not:
I know why we are not blinded
by your brightness, are able to see you,
who cannot see us. I know
why we are still here.

Godspeed.
The niggers are calculating,
from day to day, life everlasting,
and wish you well:
but decline to imitate the Son of the Morning,
and rule in Hell.

Song (for Skip)

1

I believe, my brother,
that some are haunted by a song,
all day, and all the midnight long:

I'm going to tell
God
how you treated
Me:
one of these days.

Now, if that song tormented me,
I could have no choice but be
whiter than a bleaching bone
of all the ways there are,
this must be the most dreadful
way to be alone.

White rejects light
while blackness drinks it in
becoming many colours
and stone holds heat

while grass smothers
and flowers die
and the sleeping snake
is hacked to pieces
while digesting his
(so to speak)
three-martini lunch.

Dread stalks our streets,
and our faces.
Many races
gather, again,
to despise and disperse
and destroy us:
nor can they any longer pretend
to be looking for a friend.
That dream was sold
when we were,
on the auction-block
of Manifest Destiny.

Time is not money.
Time
     is
          time.
And the time has come, again,
to outwit and outlast
survive and surmount

the authors of the blasphemy
of our chains.
At least, we know
a man, when we see one,
a shackle, when we wear one,
or a chain, when we bear one,
a noose from a halter,
or a pit from an altar.
We, who have been blinded,
are not blind
and sense when not to
trust the mind.

Time is not money.
Time is time.
You made the money.
We made the rhyme.

Our children are.
Our children are.
Our children are:
which means that we must be
the pillar of cloud by day
and of fire by night:
the guiding star.

2

My beloved brother,
I know your walk
and love to hear you
talk that talk
while your furrowed brow
grows young with wonder,
like a small boy, staring at the thunder.

I see you, somehow,
about the age of ten,
determined to enter the world of men,
yet, not too far from your mother's lap,
wearing your stunning
baseball cap.

Perhaps, then, around eleven,
wondering what to take as given,
and, not much later, going through
the agony bequeathed to you.

Then, spun around, then going under,
the small boy staring at the thunder.

Then, take it all
and use it well

this manhood, calculating
through this hell.

   3

Who says better? Who knows more
than those who enter at that door
called back
for Black,
by Christians, who
raped your mother
and, then, lynched you,
seed from their loins,
flesh of their flesh,
bone of their bone:
what an interesting way
to be alone!

Time is not money:
time is time.
And a man is a man, my brother,
and a crime remains
a crime.

The time our fathers bought for us
resides in a place no man can reach
except he be prepared

to disintegrate himself into atoms,
into smashed fragments of bleaching bone,
which is, indeed, the great temptation
beckoning this disastrous nation.
It may, indeed, precisely, be
all that they claim as History.
Those who required, of us, a song,
know that their hour is not long.

Our children are
the morning star.

Munich, Winter 1973 (for Y.S.)

In a strange house,
a strange bed
in a strange town,
a very strange me
is waiting for you.

Now
it is very early in the morning.
The silence is loud.
The baby is walking about
with his foaming bottle,
making strange sounds
and deciding, after all,
to be my friend.

You
arrive tonight.

How dull time is!
How empty—and yet,
since I am sitting here,
lying here,
walking up and down here,

waiting,
I see
that time's cruel ability
to make one wait
is time's reality.

I see your hair
which I call red.
I lie here in this bed.

Someone teased me once,
a friend of ours—
saying that I saw your hair red
because I was not thinking
of the hair on your head.

Someone also told me,
a long time ago:
my father said to me,
It is a terrible thing,
son,
to fall into the hands of the living God.
Now,
I know what he was saying.
I could not have seen red
before finding myself
in this strange, this waiting bed.
Nor had my naked eye suggested

that colour was created
by the light falling, now,
on me,
in this strange bed,
waiting
where no one has ever rested!

The streets, I observe,
are wintry.
It feels like snow.
Starlings circle in the sky,
conspiring,
together, and alone,
unspeakable journeys
into and out of the light.

I know
I will see you tonight.
And snow
may fall
enough to freeze our tongues
and scald our eyes.
We may never be found again!

Just as the birds above our heads
circling
are singing,
knowing

that, in what lies before them,
the always unknown passage,
wind, water, air,
the failing light
the falling night
the blinding sun
they must get the journey done.
Listen.
They have wings and voices
are making choices
are using what they have.
They are aware
that, on long journeys,
each bears the other,
whirring,
stirring
love occurring
in the middle of the terrifying air.

The giver (for Berdis)

If the hope of giving
is to love the living,
the giver risks madness
in the act of giving.

Some such lesson I seemed to see
in the faces that surrounded me.

Needy and blind, unhopeful, unlifted,
what gift would give them the gift to be gifted?
    The giver is no less adrift
      than those who are clamouring for the gift.

If they cannot claim it, if it is not there,
if their empty fingers beat the empty air
and the giver goes down on his knees in prayer
knows that all of his giving has been for naught
and that nothing was ever what he thought
and turns in his guilty bed to stare
at the starving multitudes standing there
and rises from bed to curse at heaven,
he must yet understand that to whom much is given
much will be taken, and justly so:
I cannot tell how much I owe.

3.00 a.m. (for David)

Two black boots,
                    on the floor,
figuring out what the walking's for.
Two black boots,
                    now, together,
learning the price of the stormy weather.

To say nothing of the wear and tear
on
      the mother-fucking
                              leather.

The darkest hour

The darkest hour
is just before the dawn,
and that, I see,
which does not guarantee
power to draw the next breath,
nor abolish the suspicion
that the brightest hour
we will ever see
occurs just before we cease
to be.

Imagination

Imagination
creates the situation,
and, then, the situation
creates imagination.

It may, of course,
be the other way around:
Columbus was discovered
by what he found.

Confession

Who knows more
of Wanda, the wan,
    than I do?
And who knows more
of Terry, the torn,
    than I do?
And who knows more
    than I do
of Ziggy, the Zap,
fleeing the rap,
using his eyes and teeth
to spring the trap,
than I do!

    Or did.

Good Lord, forbid
    that morning's acre,
held in the palm of the hand,
one's fingers helplessly returning
dust to dust,
the dust crying out,
triumphantly,
    take her!

Oh, Lord,
    can these bones live?
I think, Yes,
then I think, No:
being witness to a blow
delivered outside of time,
witness to a crime
which time
is, in no way whatever,
compelled to see,
not being burdened with sight:
    like me.

    Oh, I watch Wanda,
Wanda, the wan,
    making love with her pots,
and her frying pan:
feeding her cats,
who, never, therefore,
dream of catching the rats
who bar
her not yet barred
and most unusual door.
The cats make her wan,
    a cat
(no matter how you cut him)
    not being a man,
    or a woman, either.

And, yet,
    at that,
better than nothing:
    But
nothing is not better than nothing:
nothing is nothing,
    just like
everything is everything
(and you better believe it).

    And,
Terry, the torn,
wishes he'd never been born
because he was found sucking a cock
in the shadow of a Central Park rock.
    The cock was black,
like Terry,
and the killing, healing,
thrilling thing
was in nothing resembling a hurry:
came, just before the cops came,
and was long gone,
baby,
out of *that* park,
while the cops were writing down Terry's name.

    Well.
Birds do it.

Bees endlessly do it.
Cats leap jungles
cages and ages
to keep on doing it
and even survive
 overheated apartments
 and canned cat-food
doing it to each other
all day long.
 It is one of the many forms of love,
and, even in the cat kingdom,
of survival:
 but Wanda never looked
 and Terry didn't think he was a cat
 and he was right about that.

 Enter Ziggy, the Zap,
having taken the rap
for a friend,
fearing he was facing the end,
but very cool about it,
he thought,
selling
what others bought
(he thought).

 But Wanda had left the bazaar
tricked by a tricky star.

She knew nothing of distance,
less of light,
the star vanished
and down came night.

Wanda thought this progression natural.
Refusing to moan,
she began to drink
far too alone
to dare to think.

I watch her open door.
She thinks that she wishes
to be a whore.
But whoredom is hard work,
stinks far too much of the real,
is as ruthless as a turning wheel,
and who knows more
of this
than I do?

Oh,
      and Ziggy, the Zap,
      who took the rap,
      raps on
to his fellow prisoners
in the cell he never left
and will never leave.

You'd best believe
it's cold outside.
Nobody
        wants to go where
        nothing is everything
        and everything adds up
        to nothing.

Better to slide
into the night
cling to the memory
of the shameful rock
which watched as the shameful act occurred
yet spoke no warning
said not a word.

        And who knows more
        of shame, and rocks,
        than I do?

Oh,
        and Wanda, the wan,
        will never forgive her sky.
        That's why the old folks say
        (and who knows better than I?)
        we will understand it
        better
        by and by.

My Lord.
I understand it,
now:
the why is not the how.

My Lord,
Author of the whirlwind,
and the rainbow,
Co-author of death,
giver and taker of breath
(Yes, every knee must bow),
I understand it
now:
the why is not the how.

Le sporting-club de Monte Carlo (for Lena Horne)

The lady is a tramp
    a camp
    a lamp

The lady is a sight
    a might
    a light
the lady devastated
an alley or two
reverberated through the valley
which leads to me, and you

the lady is the apple
of God's eye:
He's cool enough about it
but He tends to strut a little
when she passes by

the lady is a wonder
daughter of the thunder
smashing cages
legislating rages
with the voice of ages
singing us through.

Some days (for Paula)

1

Some days worry
some days glad
some days
more than make you
mad.
Some days,
some days, more than
shine:
when you see what's coming
on down the line!

2

Some days you say,
oh, not me never—!
Some days you say
bless God forever.
Some days, you say,
curse God, and die
and the day comes when you wrestle

with that lie.
          Some days tussle
then some days groan
and some days
don't even leave a bone.
Some days you hassle
all alone.

   3

I don't know, sister,
what I'm saying,
nor do no man,
if he don't be praying.
I know that love is the only answer
and the tight-rope lover
the only dancer.
When the lover come off the rope
today,
the net which holds him
is how we pray,
and not to God's unknown,
but to each other—:
the falling mortal is our brother!

4

Some days leave
some days grieve
some days you almost don't believe.
Some days believe you,
some days don't,
some days believe you
and you won't.
Some days worry
some days mad
some days more than make you
glad.
Some days, some days,
more than shine,
witnesses,
coming on down the line!

Conundrum (on my birthday) (for Rico)

Between holding on,
and letting go,
I wonder
how you know
the difference.

It must be something like
the difference
between heaven and hell
but how, in advance,
can you tell?

If letting go
is saying no,
then what is holding on
saying?
 Come.
 Can anyone be held?
 Can I—?
The impossible conundrum,
the closed circle,
why
does lightning strike this house

and not another?
Or, is it true
that love is blind
until challenged by the drawbridge
of the mind?

But, saying that,
one's forced to see one's definitions
as unreal.
We do not know enough about the mind,
    or how the conundrum of the imagination
dictates, discovers,
or can dismember what we feel,
    or what we find.

Perhaps
one must learn to trust
one's terror:
the holding on
the letting go
is error:
    the lightning has no choice,
        the whirlwind has one voice.

Christmas carol

Saul,
how does it feel
to be Paul?
I mean, tell me about that night
you saw the light,
when the light knocked you down.
What's the cost
of being lost
and found?

It must be high.
And I've always thought you must have been,
stumbling homeward,
trying to find your way out of town
through all those baffling signals,
those one-way streets,
merry-making camel drivers
(complete with camels;
camels complete with loot)
going *root-a-toot-toot!*
before, and around you
and behind.
No wonder you went blind.

Like man, I can dig it.
Been there myself: you know:
it sometime happen so.
And the stink make you think
because you can't get away
you are surrounded
by the think of your stink,
unbounded.
And not just in the camels
and the drivers
and not just in the hovels
and the rivers
and not just in the sewers
where you live
and not just in the shit
beneath your nose
and not just in the dream
of getting home
and not just in the terrifying hand
which holds you tight,
forever to the land.
On such a night,
oh, yes,
one might lose sight,
fall down beneath the camels,
and see the light.

Been there myself: face down

in the mud
which rises, rises, challenging
one's mortal blood,
which courses, races, faithless,
anywhere,
which, married with the mud,
will dry at noon
soon.

Prayer
changes things.

It do.
If I can get up off this slime,
if I ain't trampled,
I will put off my former ways
I will deny my days
I will be pardoned
and I will rise
out of the camel piss
which stings my eyes
into a revelation
concerning this doomed nation.

From which I am, henceforth,
divorced forever!
Set me upon my feet,
my Lord,

I am delivered
out of the jaws of hell.
My journey splits my skull,
and, as I rise, I fall.

Get out of town.
This ain't no place to be alone.

Get past the merchants, and the shawls,
the everlasting incense: stroke your balls,
be grateful you still have them;
touch your prick
in a storm of wondering abnegation:
it will be needed no longer,
the light being so much stronger.

Get out of town
Get out of town
Get out of town

And don't let nobody
turn you around.

Nobody will: for they see, too,
 how the hand of the Lord has been laid on you.
    Ride on!
Let the drivers stare
and the camel's farts define the air.

Ride on!
Don't be deterred, man,
for the crown ain't given to the also-ran.

Oh, Saul,
how does it feel to be Paul?

Sometimes I wonder about that night.
One does not always walk in light.
My light is darkness
and in my darkness moves, forever,
the dream or the hope or the fear of sight.

Ride on!
     This hand, sometimes, at the midnight hour,
yearning for land, strokes a growing power,
true believer!
     Will he come again?
When will my Lord send my roots rain?
Will he hear my prayer?
     Oh, man, don't fight it
Will he clothe my grief?
     Man, talk about it
That night, that light
     Baby, now you coming.
I will be uncovered, on that morning,
     And I'll be there.

No tongue can stammer
nor hammer ring
no leaf bear witness
to how bright is the light
of the unchained night
which delivered
Saul
to Paul.

A lady like landscapes (for Simone Signoret)

A lady like landscapes,
wearing time like an amusing shawl
thrown over her shoulders
by a friend at the bazaar:

Every once in a while she turns in it
just like a little girl,
this way and that way:

Regarde.
Ça n'était pas donné bien sûr
mais c'est quand même beau, non?

Oui, Oui.
Et toi aussi.
Ou plutôt belle
since you are a lady.

It is impossible to tell
how beautiful, how real, unanswerable,
becomes your landscape as you move in it,
how beautiful the shawl.

Guilt, Desire and Love

At the dark street corner
where Guilt and Desire
are attempting to stare
each other down
(presently, one of them
will light a cigarette
and glance in the direction
of the abandoned warehouse)
Love came slouching along,
an exploded silence
standing a little apart
but visible anyway
in the yellow, silent, steaming light,
while Guilt and Desire wrangled,
trying not to be overheard
by this trespasser.

Each time Desire looked towards Love,
hoping to find a witness,
Guilt shouted louder
and shook them hips
and the fire of the cigarette
threatened to burn the warehouse down.

Desire actually started across the street,
time after time,
to hear what Love might have to say,
but Guilt flagged down a truckload
of other people
and knelt down in the middle of the street
and, while the truckload of other people
looked away, and swore that they
didn't see nothing
and couldn't testify nohow,
and Love moved out of sight,
Guilt accomplished upon the standing body
of Desire
the momentary, inflammatory soothing
which seals their union
(for ever?)
and creates a mighty traffic problem.

Death is easy (for Jefe)

1

Death is easy.
One is compelled to understand
that moment
which, anyway, occurs
over and over and over.
Lord,
sitting here now,
with my boy with a toothache
in the bed yonder,
asleep, I hope,
and me, awake,
so far away,
cursing the toothache,
cursing myself,
cursing the fence
of pain.

2

Pain is not easy;
reduces one to

toothaches
which may or may not
be real,
but which are real
enough
to make one sleep,
or wake,
or decide
that death is easy.

3

It is dreadful to be
so violently dispersed.
To dare hope for nothing,
and yet dare to hope.
To know that hoping
and not hoping
are both criminal endeavours,
and, yet, to play one's cards.

4

If
I could tell you
anything about myself:

if I knew something
useful—:
if I could ride,
master,
the storm of the unknown
me,
well, then, I could prevent
the panic of toothaches.
If I knew
something,
if I could recover
something,
well, then,
I could kiss the toothache
away,
and be with my lover,
who doesn't, after all,
like toothaches.

5

Death is easy
when,
if,
love dies.
Anguish is the no-man's-land
focused in the eyes.

Mirrors (for David)

1

Although you know
what's best for me,
I cannot act on what you see.
I wish I could:
I really would,
          and joyfully,
act out my salvation
with your imagination.

2

Although I may not see your heart,
or fearful well-springs of your art,
I know enough to stare
down danger, anywhere.
I know enough to tell
you to go to hell
and when I think you're wrong
I will not go along.
I have a right to tremble

when you begin to crumble.
Your life is my life, too,
and nothing you can do
will make you something other
than my mule-headed brother.

A Lover's Question

My country,
'tis of thee
I sing.

You, enemy of all tribes,
known, unknown, past,
present, or,
perhaps, above all,
to come:
I sing:
my dear,
          my darling,
jewel
(*Columbia, the gem of
the ocean!*)
or, as I, a street nigger,
would put it—:
(Okay. I'm *your* nigger
baby, till I get bigger!)
You are my heart.

Why
have you allowed yourself
to become so *grimly* wicked?

I
do not ask you why
you have spurned,
despised my love
as something beneath you.
We all have our ways and
days
but my love has been as constant
as the rays
coming from the earth
or the sun,
which you have used to obliterate
me,
and, now, according to your purpose,
all mankind,
from the nigger, to you,
and to your children's children.

I have endured your fire
and your whip,
your rope,
and the panic from your hip,
in many ways, false lover,
yet, my love:
you do not know
how desperately I hoped
that you would grow
not so much to love me
as to know
that what you do to me
you do to you.

No man can have a harlot
for a lover
nor stay in bed forever
with a lie.
He must rise up
and face the morning sky
and himself, in the mirror
of his lover's eye.

You do not love me.
I see that.
You do not see me:
I am your black cat.

You forget
that I remember an Egypt
where I was worshipped
where I was loved.

No one has ever worshipped you,
nor ever can: you think that love
is a territorial matter,
and racial,
oh, yes,
where I was worshipped
and you were hurling stones,
stones which you have hurled at me,
to kill me,
and, now,
you hurl at the earth,

our mother,
the toys which slaughtered
Cain's brother.

What panic makes you
want to die?
How can you fail to look
into your lover's eye?

Your black dancer
holds the answer:
your only hope
beyond the rope.

Of rope you fashioned,
usefully,
enough hangs from
your hanging tree
to carry you
where you sent me.

And, then, false lover,
you will know
what love has managed
here below.

Inventory/On Being 52

My progress report
concerning my journey to the palace of wisdom
is discouraging.
I lack certain indispensable aptitudes.
Furthermore, it appears
that I packed the wrong things.
I thought I packed what was necessary,
or what little I had:
but there is always something one overlooks,
something one was not told,
or did not hear.

Furthermore,
some time ago,
I seem to have made an error in judgment,
turned this way, instead of that,
and, now, I cannot radio my position.
(I am not sure that my radio is working.
No voice has answered me for a long time now.)

How long?
I do not know.

It may have been
that day, in Norman's Gardens,
up-town, somewhere,
when I did not hear
someone trying to say: I love you.
I packed for the journey in great haste.
I have never had any time to spare.
I left behind me
all that I could not carry.

I seem to remember, now,
a green bauble, a worthless stone,
slimy with the rain.
My mother said that I should take it with me,
but I left it behind.
(The world is full of green stones, I said.)

Funny
that I should think of it now.
I never saw another one like it —:
now, that I think of it.

There was a red piece of altar-cloth,
which had belonged to my father,
but I was much too old for it,
and I left it behind.

There was a little brown ball,
belonging to a neighbor's little boy.
I still remember his face,
brown, like the ball, and shining like the sun,
the day he threw it to me
and I caught it
and turned my back, and dropped it,
and left it behind.

I was on my way.
Drums and trumpets called me.
My universe was thunder.
My eye was fixed
on the far place of the palace.

But, sometimes, my attention was distracted
by this one, or that one,
by a river, by the cry of a child,
the sound of chains,
of howling. Sometimes
the wings of great birds
flailed my nostrils,
veiled my face, sometimes,
from high places, rocks fell on me,
sometimes, I was distracted by my blood,
rushing over my palm,
fouling the lightning of my robe.

My father's son
does not easily surrender.

My mother's son
pressed on.

Then,
I began to imagine a strange thing:
the palace never came any closer.
I began, nervously, to check
my watch, my compass, the stars:
they all confirmed
that I was almost certainly where I should be.
The vegetation was proper
for the place, and the time of year.
The flowers were dying,
but that, I knew,
was virtual, at this altitude.
It was cold,
but I was walking upward, toward the sun,
and it was silent, but—
silence and I have always been friends.

Yet—
my journey's end seemed
farther
than I had thought it would be.

I feel as though I have been badly bruised.
I hope that there is no internal damage.
I seem to be awakening
from a long, long fall.

My radio will never work again.
My compass has betrayed me.
My watch has stopped.

Perhaps
I will never find my way to the palace.
Certainly,
I do not know which way to turn.

My progress has been
discouraging.

Perhaps
I should locate the turning
and then start back
and study the road I've travelled.
Oh, I was in a hurry,
but it was not, after all,
if I remember,
an ugly road at all.
Sometimes, I saw
wonders greater than any palace,
yes,
and, sometimes, joy leaped out,
mightier than the lightning of my robe,
and kissed my nakedness.
Songs
came out of rocks and stones and chains,
wonder baptized me,
old trees sometimes opened, and let me in,

and led me along their roots,
down, to the bottom of the rain.

The green stone,
the scarlet altar-cloth,
the brown ball, the brown boy's face,
the voice, in Norman's Gardens,
trying to say: I love you.

Yes.
My progress has been discouraging.
But I think I will leave the palace where it is.
It has taken up quite enough of my time.
The compass, the watch, and the radio:
I think I will leave them here.
I think I know the road, by now,
and, if not, well, I'll certainly think of something.
Perhaps the stars will help,
or the water,
a stone may have something to tell me,
and I owe a favor to a couple of old trees
And what was that song I learned from the river
on one of those dark days?
If I can remember the first few notes
Yes
I think it went something like
Yes
It may have been the day I met the howling man,

who looked at me so strangely.
He wore no coat.
He said perhaps he'd left it at Norman's Gardens,
up-town, someplace.
Perhaps, this time, should we meet again, I'll
stop and rap a little.
A howling man may have discovered something I should
   know,
something, perhaps, concerning my discouraging progress.

This time, however,
hopefully,
should the voice hold me to tarry,
I'll be given what to carry.

Amen

No, I don't feel death coming.
I feel death going:
having thrown up his hands,
for the moment.

I feel like I know him
better than I did.
Those arms held me,
for a while,
and, when we meet again,
there will be that secret knowledge
between us.

OTHER
POEMS

Gypsy

He was standing at the bath-room mirror,
shaving,
had just stepped out of the shower,
naked,
balls retracted, prick limped out of the
small,
morning hard-on,
thinking of nothing but foam and steam,
when the bell
rang.

Not knowing why,
for no reason,
he touched his balls
and heard his wife,
Elizabeth,
call, *coming!*

Then, he heard the children,
Joe, five,
Pam, three
(They had, more or less,
been planned),
giggling and conspiring

at the breakfast table.
(They seemed to be happy:
with more to say to each other
than they ever said to him.)
And, then, as he tied the towel
at his waist,
he seemed to hear a kind of
groaning
in his house
A kind of moaning, even,
and he looked at himself
in the mirror,
and, for no reason,
he was, suddenly:
afraid.
He looked at himself,
seeing the face he had
always
and never seen:
not a bad face,
pink, now, from the steam,
laboring through the fog of the mirror,
to be scrutinized.
Assessed,
one more time.
No, not a bad face at all

cheek-bones high,
a cleft in the chin,
wide mouth, lips that loved
to open,
to suck, to close,
to laugh,
big straight teeth,
broad, wide-nostriled nose,
high fore-head,
curly black hair,
the face of a Gypsy Jew
And he was, indeed,
Sephardic,
and had loved Spain,
when he had walked
and gawked,
there,
years before he had become
American.

Elizabeth now called him
again.
And he was afraid,
again,
not knowing why,
and angry at himself

for not knowing
why
he was afraid.
Coming!
he called, again,
and, then, in the bed-room,
putting on his shorts,
looking for his shirt,
he called,
What is it?

And Elizabeth came into the
bed-room,
looking as nice as she always
looked to him,
and looking frightened.
She said,
There are some men here
to see you,
from the FBI.
The FBI?
That's what they said.
He laughed,
as he got into his trousers.
She helped him with his shirt.
If that don't beat all!

But, he realized, suddenly,
that Joe and Pam were not talking,
anymore,
and Elizabeth, abruptly, left him,
and he put on his shoes.
He put on his watch.
It said: eight-thirty.
He was to remember that.

One was standing in the kitchen.
One was standing in the living-room.
The one in the kitchen
stood too close to the children.
He did not like the way
this man looked at his children.
He did not like the way this man
looked at Elizabeth.
He did not like the way the man
in the living room
looked at his books,
holding one in his hands
as though it were reptilian,
putting it down on the table
as though the room were a swamp.
Yet, if he had seen them
on the train to work,

in the streets, in a bar,
he wouldn't have noticed them at all.
They looked perfectly ordinary,
dressed as safely as he was
dressed.
Anonymous, and, above all,
democratic.

You are?
This was the one in the kitchen.
It was not a question.
It was a statement containing
contempt.
He felt the blood hit his temples.
He put his hands in his pockets,
trembling.
He said, *What's this about?*
But his voice was another man's
voice.
He did not recognize his voice.
His voice:
now, he realized that he had never
heard his voice.
The one in the living-room
picked up another book,
dropped it,

said,
We're asking the questions.
Mister.
Came into the kitchen
and patted little Joe on the head.
Joe jumped up and ran to his
father,
who put one trembling arm around him,
and said,
I think I have a right to ask
questions.
What are you doing in my house?
What do you want?
They flashed badges.
He said,
That don't mean shit.
They laughed. Pam began to cry.
Elizabeth went to her,
staring at the men.
Oh yes, it does,
the living-room man said,
And you are in it.
The kitchen man laughed.
He produced a photograph.
He seemed to take it out of his hat
Though his hat was on the kitchen table.

When did you last see this man,
Mister?

He wanted to say,
I do not know this man.
He stared at a photograph of a man
who had been his teacher, once,
a very fine man.
A very fine teacher.
His name was Stone.

I have not seen him in some time,
he said,
cold, now, and angry in another way,
and too relieved to know what this was
about, frightened
to be, for the moment, anymore.
Then, the living-room man said:
And you signed this?
And took out an old, rolled-up piece of
paper,
like a scroll,
and thrust it at him.
He read,
Genocide is among the American crimes,
and we petition this nation to
atone.

He looked at this for a long time.
He remembered signing it: he did not
look for his name.
He ran his hands through his son's
abruptly electric hair,
and stared at the living-room man,
and the kitchen man,
and said,
Yes. I signed it. You know that.
Why are you here?
The kitchen man said,
Your teacher wrote a book, too, didn't he?
He said, *Yes.* Then, *Not a bad book,*
either.
He was beginning to tremble.
He wanted to laugh.
He felt his son clasp his thigh.
The living-room man said,
Well, he's in jail, your teacher.
He was a faggot Commie spy.
The kitchen man said,
I bet he made out with you,
You, with your cute round ass.
Yeah. That's why you signed this
garbage.
He willed his thigh not to tremble

against his son's head.
He said, *Why are you here?*
And they said, together,
We got some questions to ask you!
Then. Elizabeth asked,
Are you arresting my husband?
And they said, together,
Yeah. Come on, Buster. Move it.

He woke up. The door-bell rang.

Song For The Shepherd Boy

What wouldn't I give
to be with you.

Hey. The rags of my life are few.
Abandoned priceless gems are scattered
here and there
I don't know where—
never expected to have them,
much less need them,
but, now, an ache, like the beginning
of the rain,
makes me wonder where they are.

If I knew, I would go there,
travelling far and far
and find them
to give them to you.

You
would be amazed.
I see your amber color raised
and those eyes—!
brighter than the jewels, far
more amazing than the loot
of my looted life.

Well. Then.
There is my pain.
I never thought to think
of it again.
And pain's no gift
it will not lift
you up from the mid-night hour.
Pain cannot be given,
can only be tracked down,
discovered
somewhere—somewhere within that catacomb,
that maze, that dungeon,
which my breath built,
and in which I begin to move,
now,
        searching
for something to give to you.

May '86, Amherst
(for David)

For A.

Sitting in the house, with everything on my mind.
Stumbling in my house, watching my lover go stone-blind.

Come back from that window. Please don't open that door!
I know where it leads. It leads to hell, and more
than your blinded eyes can see. Come back,
come back, and try to lean on me.
I'm here, I'm here, I've gone nowhere away:
if only you could see!

How is it we have travelled, you and me,
through happy days, and torment, and not guessed
that we could find ourselves so black, unblessed,
so far apart?
You are my heart:
I watched you sleep and watched you play.
I slapped your buttocks every day.
I used to laugh with you when you laughed
and stand, when you stood up, and, with you,
watched the land drop down beneath us,
green and brown and crooked,
as we rose up, up into a sky
which we alone had found
and where we were alone. Too much alone, perhaps.
Perhaps we were as wicked as people said,
turning to each other for the living bread!

And, now: I have taken your hope away, you say,
and you think of me, sometimes, as the most
monstrous of old men. No matter:
if I could only make you see
how you must live when you are far away from me.
If only I could see for you, if I could for you spell
the vast contours of hell!
If I could tell you how, on such a road,
where I walked once, I stumbled and fell and howled:
how you must walk the road, and not be driven
into the great wilderness, by some false dream of heaven!
I have been there, and I know. But I know, too,
that nothing I say now will get to you.
You have your journey now, and I have mine.
And all day and all night long
I have waited for a sign
which will not be given to us now.

Love,
love has no gifts to give
except the revelation that the soul can live:
on a coming day,
you will hear, from afar,
I, your lover, pray.
You will hear, then, the prayer that you cannot hear now,
and, when you hear that sobbing, boy, rejoice,
and know that love is the purpose of the human voice!

Neuilly s/Seine
July 23, 1970

For EARL

I wish I had known more
than love ever knows, in time.
One imagines that time
gives the time
to quarrel,
correct, tyrannize,
and love.

Baby brother,
the light of your passage
has become the light in my own:
and I had planned it, *bambino*,
quite the other way around.

Enough. So much for plans.
Enough of calculations.
I will never see you
as I saw you,
again,
never touch you or kiss you
or scold you again.

You were very patient with me
very loving

but I was sure that I would die before you
and wanted you to be able to live without me.
So much for calculations.
So much for wisdom.
So much for age.
You have humbled me, my friend,
who, now, must learn to live without you.

I will miss, forever,
your eyes, your walk,
your talk—enough

My friend, Miss Lena Horne,
and many other saints
sing you, my darling,
into the womb of eternity.
Therefore, farewell,
                    for now:
Dig you, later: alligator.

Untitled

Lord,

        when you send the rain,

        think about it, please,

        a little?

  Do

        not get carried away

        by the sound of falling water,

        the marvelous light

        on the falling water.

   I

        am beneath that water.

        It falls with great force

        and the light

Blinds

        me to the light.

BALLAD (for Yoran)

I

Started to leave
and couldn't go
for a Yes
or for a No.

Watched the silver tracks turn black
as my lover's back.
Stood there through the night
watched the black turn white.

Started to leave, but couldn't go:
for a Yes, or for a No.

Heard the thunder,
saw his face,
lightning played around the place
where I stood, and couldn't go
for a Yes, or for a No.

II

The hardest thing of all
is hearing the silence fall—
or, no, to see it,
touch it,
watch silence take a form,
watch silence proudly stride
between connecting rooms,
hear silence ride
between, between,
between
you, and all others,
you
and
you.

Oh, Brother, say:
I couldn't hear nobody pray.

III

The silence coming yonder
is far from grief
and brings relief.
Beyond time
there is no wonder
there is no crime.

they say:

Brother,
just between me and you
tell me if it's true!

They say
silence brings no anguish
where only silence lives:
negatives,
affirmatives.

During his lifetime (1924–1987), **JAMES BALDWIN** authored seven novels, as well as several plays and essay collections, which were published to widespread praise. These books, among them *Notes of a Native Son*, *The Fire Next Time*, *Giovanni's Room*, and *Go Tell It on the Mountain*, brought him well-deserved acclaim as a public intellectual and admiration as a writer. However, Baldwin's earliest writing was in poetic form, and Baldwin considered himself a poet throughout his lifetime. Nonetheless, his single book of poetry, *Jimmy's Blues*, never achieved the popularity of his novels and nonfiction, and is the one and only book to fall out of print.

NIKKY FINNEY has authored four books of poetry, including *Head Off & Split*, which was awarded the 2011 National Book Award for poetry. She is currently the John H. Bennett, Jr., Chair in Southern Letters and Creative Writing at the University of South Carolina.